PATRICIA McGOVERN

THE CAREER THAT ATE MY LIFE

*Tough Love
For Single Women
Who Wonder Where
Their Dreams Went!*

Lulu

CONTENTS

CHAPTER 1 – CATALYST

Flashback 1980's style. Big hair, power suits, shoulder pads, lotsa gold.

Women were scaling the corporate ladder like Green Beret commandos dressed in silk fatigues, sporting cherry lip gloss.

MONEY   INDEPENDENCE   EXCESS

Everything going gang busters.

Magazines and television shows lighting the beacons, beckoning for young women to follow the charge.

Icons of an era.

THE NEW BREED.

If you were just leaving high school or university around this time, you couldn't help but be swept up in this exciting opportunity, ready to jump on the corporate bandwagon….the path to…..SUCCESS.

And so we did.

Worldwide.

Storming past the eighties and into the nineties hell for leather.

Unquestioning.

Partying through our twenties with wads of spare cash and lighting the candles on our thirtieth birthday cakes.

By now we were moving into the senior ranks of our chosen fields, propped up by our go-getter *women's* magazines and financial advisors.

Busy schedules, long hours.

FOCUS, FOCUS, FOCUS.

And confidence!

Achievement.

Rewards.

Hard work.

Boyfriends came and went.

ENTER : The New Millennium.

The all important money flow continued to build.

Addictive.

Unrelenting.

Taken for granted.

Call it age, call it maturity, call it burn out, but at some point on the ride I had a burning realization that I wanted to jump off.

The pedestal began to tilt.

My perception of *success*, our achievements and aspirations, started to change.

The Career That Ate My Life

Gone from my thoughts was the notion that life
was centered around an office building.

Yes we had achieved, but what did we truly have to
show for our lives besides the latest handbag?

Did I jump off?

No. Well sort of.

I kept the dollars flowing but started to choose my
jobs a little differently.

I started to wonder if being at the top was all worth
it, or if I'd even get there without selling my soul
or because of my gender.

So no, I didn't really jump off.

Neither did my friends.

Year by year, the number of friends with hot men
on their heels dwindled.

I noticed my gal pals had developed into two
distinct categories.

Those that had more one-night boyfriends than
they could remember and those that barely moved
beyond first base with men.

They were all seemingly too busy to be committed
or just weren't meeting the *right* type of guys.

Their common ingredient was that neither group was forming solid, long lasting relationships with the opposite sex.

One group discarding anyone who came too close on an emotional level, and the other seemingly unable to move beyond the type of awkward banter and giggling post-mortems we were all part of at the local high school dances twenty years earlier.

In past years everyone had appeared to be totally at ease with this scenario.

They had solid social groups who stuck by them whether on long drinking nights or quiet, reflective weekends.

But over time, faces started to change.

Gone was the inspired glint in their eyes when they talked about 'the one'.

An honest, childlike, bewildered look came across their faces that made me question what was really happening behind the happy facades.

Were my friends as content with their lives as they made out, or were they just sticking to the life they knew because they didn't know where else to go?

Every other topic of conversation remained bright and brilliant over many a long gossip-filled lunch.

But the smile cracked ever so slightly when *the future* was a point of discussion.

As I pondered and posed the questions in my own mind, it became clear.

My friends, their friends, sisters, cousins were collectively forming into what felt like an ever-growing group of people who weren't going to be finding a long term partner any time soon.

A quiet phenomenon was creeping into our social spectrum.

These were the ***lost girls***….the faces of children who assumed they'd follow in their mothers' footsteps and be married with children and a 'full' life at some stage, only that stage didn't seem to be anywhere on the horizon….not even close.

That leads me to us.

YOU and ME.

CHAPTER 2 –

CAN SOMEONE PLEASE SWITCH THE LIGHT ON?

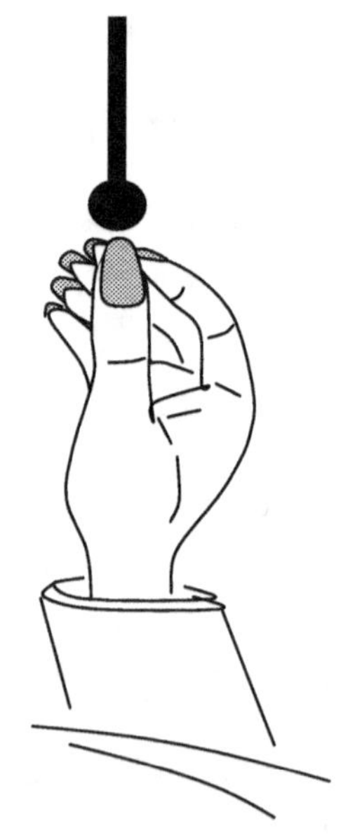

So let me describe you my friend, as you are today.

You're now a busy woman in your thirties or forties with a hectic schedule that requires a mammoth commitment, great coordination and pretty strong discipline.

We know your history. You've been in a responsible job since you left high school or university, working hard and gaining respect amongst your peers or industry colleagues.

Your twenties were awesome.

You had your share of wild nights, parties, fun, flings and relationships, but your career has been your focus.

You've had to sacrifice personal time to do well and you've been prepared to do it.

Somewhere along the line your career has gained more and more significance to the point where you've allowed it to define a large part of

WHO YOU ARE.

It's never far from your lips as a point of discussion with anyone you meet.

It's highly important to you that any prospective partner understand and respect what you do.

You're busy and he needs to fit in around that for any relationship to work.

Ok, we've established you're a successful career woman with a healthy bank balance or a closet full of designer shoes and clothes, maybe your own apartment, a car.

You've done well and should be proud of it!

So why are you here?

What do you want that you don't already have?

You want the husband, the kids,

'THE LIFE'.

You want to fulfill all those dreams you had when you were ten years old and assumed would come to fruition.

So before we go any further, I have to ask you to do a favor for me.

STOP.

CHAPTER 3 – STOP

I need you to stop and acknowledge something.

I want you to be honest with yourself.

The truth.

Your life…

…right now…

…is empty.

I'm sure you have an array of social activities lined up to fill your days….off to the races with friends, drinks at a launch party, lots of laughs on a regular basis.

But deep inside – you know the spot where the *real* you lies – there's a void, an unnerving, gut wrenching feeling that you're unable to shake.

The one that tells you **'this is all wrong'**.

What's wrong with it?

There's no one of significance in it...

...and nothing significant...

...TO YOU...

...about it.

You have a multitude of friends, you might play a few sports or visit heaps of galleries…..all good stuff.

But there's no one even *close* to significant in it is there?

Beyond the horizon, there's no one even in your stratosphere. The tank is beyond dry. The drought is beyond El Nino.

"Ouch!! Steady on!! There might not be a man or kids in my life, but don't tell me there's nothing happening for me!"

"What are you? An ultra conservative, anti-career, bare-foot-and-pregnant, women-as-doormats advocate?"

I hear you say.

No….to all those things.

You're misinterpreting me. I'm not saying you are a nothing or nobody for not being married with ten children.

What I'm saying is that in YOUR WORLD…..where you are right now…..your LIFE does NOT resemble your DREAMS.

Instead, it's an endless groundhog day of work – getting to work…staying back late to finish that document that's due tomorrow… thinking about work endlessly when you're not at work… going in to the office on a public holiday… thinking about which job you'd like to do next and who you can network with to get it… obsessing about how annoyed you are at your peer for side swiping you in a meeting yesterday.

Am I right or am I right?

How do I know?

Because I'd be lying if I said I hadn't experienced exactly the same thing, to some degree, at some point in my life.

Don't forget, I was there too.

If any of this looks like you, then I need to tell you something.

Your life has OFFICIALLY been EATEN by your CAREER.

Yep. Sorry to break it to you but you're in the hole.

(Answer Quiz 1 to see how deep in the hole you are – see appendix!)

And while you're in the hole, as dark as it is, let's agree another point of truth.

You *want* 'the life'

You want all those things you dreamt about when you're were a little girl. Sure you may have

tweaked them a little to take them out of girlie
thoughts and into sophisticated woman-speak.

You want 'the life'
….you don't have it,
…you don't know how to get it,
…and you're really starting to question whether
you will ever find it.

CLUNK

I just heard your jaw hit the floor.

Sorry.

I hate to be the bearer of bad news.

Can I tell you something positive now? Something
to make that jaw pick up ever so slightly from the
polished floorboards?

DON'T WORRY(-ish)

Don't worry…we're gonna find a way to get things
back on track for you.…starting today.

I'm not saying don't worry *at all*, because we do
need to worry somewhat.

I just mean don't feel like this hole you're in is so
deep you'll never get out of it.

Don't turn in to an obsessed blithering mess of
worry.

Just note this is a REALLY BIG DEAL …
….AND…..we're going to turn our concern into
affirmative action.

Not a big deal just for today.

This is probably the BIGGEST deal….ever….and
we can change it.

Now *that's* going to take a bit of doing. Because
you see you've spent the last however many
years…a lot of your adult life…going down a path
you thought was the right one,

only to agree today,

two minutes ago,

that it maybe hasn't quite lead you to where you
thought it might.

That sucks the big one doesn't it?

I mean how often are you wrong about stuff you do
in your job….probably not often I bet.

But to now look at the last fifteen to twenty years
of our lives and decide that the road we took….that
material world we read about in the glossy
magazines as being 'the ultimate'…..money, cars,
assets, prestige, freedom, holidays (nothing wrong
with any of them)….all the stuff we heard on
television about power women….that we've lapped

it up, sloshed it round in our minds and turned us in to…

US!

So we do have some work to do.

So don't worry-(ish).

Keep reading on, once you've thrown this book in the fire…and then retrieved it.…jumped on it a few times or rung out your wet tissues on it.

"Don't worry she says.…are you kidding me? You've just pulled me apart, limb from limb, ripped out my heart, called me a *'lost girl'* and told me that I've made what appears to me to be a profound life mistake, but hey.…according to YOU everything's going to be ok."

"Well thanks for that.…

I feel ***soooo*** much better now!"

You should.

We'll do it.

It may not come out exactly as you'd planned, but it's a damn site better from where you are now isn't it?

I mean ten minutes ago you hadn't consciously contemplated this.

And MISTAKE is the wrong word.

You've done your best, based on what those 1980's and 90's beacons of light flagged as the right way to go.

You were a moth to the flame. Maybe a butterfly is better word.

You are part of a seismic shift never before experienced in the history of the world. Women have never had more money, more power… and more pressure.

So you have a choice to stick with this or not.

Let's give it a good shot now anyway….you can burn this book ONCE you've read it.

I'm not saying the new road is going to be easy at first…maybe more like a marathon than a walk in the park, but you're going in to training right now.

Not great on the exercise?

LEARN TO BE.

Given that you've done pretty well in your business life to date, you're used to doing things a certain way to gain the best outcome.

Right?

Ok, this is a little different.

We both know you can mould and shape your career with the best of 'em, and you're pretty good at planning out next moves.

So we'll use some of those skills.

But this is something a little harder to control and acquire. We're talking meeting the right man…for you….and it ending happily ever after.

If you were handed a project with that objective, how would you rate it?

Easy, moderate, complex?

Depends on you. But fair to say, like anything, a daunting project if you don't put 110% of preparation, effort and sustained focus into it.

Or you might be of the ilk that thinks…

"It's fate…isn't it?"

"It's out of your hands isn't it?"

"I mean it's just going to happen when the time's right isn't it?"

Or not?

Hasn't yet, so if you think things can stay as is and it'll all work out….fine, that's ok. What are your odds…….50,000 to one?

Maybe less….maybe more.

Up to you whichever way you think, but I'd prefer to go proactive now and tempt fate rather than putting on the nanna nightie and telling fate to put it back in his pants.

Wouldn't you?

So STOP.

Stop…..pretending to yourself and the outside world that you don't want it

Stop…..thinking it's just gonna happen

Stop…..telling me that career really is enough

Stop…..beating yourself up about not yet finding it.

Stop…pretending you don't want it.

I've been friends with a lot of gals for a lot of years, and it amazes me how much each of us has either pretended or minimized the fact that we want 'the life'.

I've done it a million times over.

It just wasn't popular or sophisticated to say that's what you're after.

We say the word *baby* like it's a disease. And sometimes it's dangerous to mention stuff like that with work colleagues for fear of missing a promotion or not being taken seriously.

But seriously…..if you continue pretending, you'll continue to rob yourself of the future you're after.

That doesn't mean you have to walk in to your boss on Monday morning and let him know this is the 'new you'.

Subtlety is ok.

But the more you can use your network of contacts – family, friends, associates to get out and meet people…particularly if they know you're in the market…

…hey not desperate, just available….

then you stand a much greater chance of meeting someone significant than if you hide your thoughts in the glory box of shame.

It took one of my friends about four years of figuratively beating up on other women who had chosen that path to finally admit to me that's what she was desperate for.

I remember one time she mentioned that a woman at work was pregnant, and in the same breath smirked that her colleague was now neatly 'out of the running for that new job' everyone was vying for.

I think her words were 'one less competitor'. So much for sisterhood!

A few months after finally admitting she wanted a family, she quit her high paying corporate-ladder job and was on a plane to London to find her own version of 'the life'…..she couldn't wait any longer and she wasn't finding it where she was.

So I'm giving you permission….it's ok to say you want it.

It's ok to shout it out
and say you x$)@(* want it.

Why?

Because it's inherently human that's why.

It cuts to the core of who we are as women.

We've spent so long suppressing it that we actually need to dig around and find it to remember who we are and what we want!

Pretty sad really.

Hey but we're not into sadness now…enough of that…it's all blue skies from here.

Stop…thinking it's just gonna happen.

Raise your hand if you've fallen into this one too.

For some of us it's about finding a man.

For others it's about pushing the family wagon to the back of the train, floating along blissfully, sniggering at the articles that talk about body clocks, and having the internal arrogance to assume it'll be alright on the night…..if and when we choose to do something about it.

Well let me tell you - nature, destiny, *whatever* will show you a thing or two about when stuff's gonna happen.

Don't just assume because you're fit, healthy and feeling great that you can control the natural physiological world.

Our business worlds become so scheduled and manicured that we assume our organic, natural lives will fit the same mould.

…and we're wrong.

We talk about being these earthy 'goddesses' and we couldn't be further from that fantasy if we tried.

We're less in touch with our natural selves than we've ever been.

We're covered in stockings and business shirts and PDA's. We're all about structure, meetings, time poor, health starved burn out…..wow, how attractive must we be to the opposite sex?

<u>Stop…telling me that career really is enough</u>

When you're twenty-two, full of energy and willing to do any mundane task because you just want to please, then work can be an exciting journey.

Try ten or twenty years later after you've been hauling your butt up that rubbery ladder, working long days and talking to absolute goobers just to get the next promotion, and you may feel a little differently.

Look I'm not saying that a good job can't be great…...it can be stimulating and it gives us the dollars to do what we want, whether it's travel, cars, investments, you name it.

But keep it in perspective…..I've always said it's no good owning a Porsche if all you do is park it under your office building.

And if you happen to be a *twenty-something* reading this and rolling on the floor with laughter over those silly Generation X women who were foolish enough to get themselves in to this situation, let me just ask you to pick yourself up off that floor and do a few things for us.

With love, from Generation X...to Generation Y :

- If you have a man you love today, don't make work the priority over your relationship. Sounds easier to juggle than it is. You can always get a new job but maybe there's only *the one* soul mate for you. And you don't want to find that out *after* you've broken up.

- If you're offered a fabulous opportunity that will mean you're away a lot, with long hours...but he'll understand....if you really want your relationship to work you'll think ten times....not just twice....before you take it.

- If you meet someone you really like and you're just finding it a little too difficult to fit in a date around your calendars, throw your electronic diary in the ocean and call him now to see if he's free.

- And if you haven't met anyone significant yet....and you really want to....MAKE IT YOUR NUMBER ONE PRIORITY

TODAY. BLAST OPEN THE DOOR.

You're only in your twenties once, and it's great, great fun to share that time with someone special. Now back to our regular listeners.

<u>Stop…beating yourself up about it</u>

If all of this sounds too familiar by now, you may be feeling sick or freaked out at the fact that

YOU ARE HERE.

You know what? Don't.

You're not an idiot, a screw up, a failure or a loser.

You haven't done anything 'wrong'. You've just steered your life off the course you originally intended…like many other women worldwide.

Like I said, it's the times….the era.

Many of us are either the product of mothers who were housebound and wanted their daughters to have more choices….or the product of the divorce era that meant we really wanted to give ourselves security.

But enough of history….it's what you do NOW that will set you apart from the masses and determine whether

YOU GET WHAT YOU WANT

or end up spending a few more years hanging out for 'movie nights' with your pals.

From here this is where it gets tricky.
You and I are gonna talk about some things soon that may make you excited about the future or rip out these pages in disgust.

There are things I'm going to say to you that may make you think I'm not on your side….like I'm attacking your very ethos.

Like I'm attacking WOMEN.

Am I? No.

What I am doing is voicing my opinion on the way we as career women sometimes think and act that I believe heavily impacts our chances of finding the happiness we've agreed you're searching for.

If that type of discussion's not for you, that's ok.

Whichever way you go, the aim is to instill activity…

…an URGENCY in you to change some things in your life and focus on …

…THE END GAME…

'the life' you want.

So keep working through these pages and decide what works for you.

Every journey is different, and the only one who can decide your path is you.

Forget about your path to date.

Forget about where each decision may have made the difference between dream and harsh reality.

Close that road and start walking through the garden.

Get cracking and make your life a full and happy one!

So here we go.

CHAPTER 4 –

MEN ARE FROM HEAVEN

(A.K.A. 'BIG NOSE')

If I haven't heard it a hundred times……

"He wanted to hang out with me ALL day, but I already said I'd go see some real estate with one of my friends who's looking to buy, so I told him to call me later"…

"He didn't ring me until Thursday, when he should have called by Wednesday latest. That's just not on with me"…

"I was too busy to talk and he knows not to bother me when I'm working on a proposal"…

"We shagged. Then I heard through one of my friends he was out talking to this other girl. So I figured why bother?"….

"I didn't like his furniture AT ALL. It was really cheap and the pieces didn't work together. He doesn't have enough style"……

"When he didn't ring I decided I'd had enough so I called him and just confronted him about it"….

"I like him but….he has a big nose…..so I'm not sure if I'd go out with him"….

Excuse me?

Have we listened to ourselves lately?

So we expect :

- ***Men to read our minds***….does he *know* you're interested…beyond the one- or two-nighter? Should he *assume* what times of day or night you might want to be with him? Did you ever think of asking him out?

- ***Guys to know….and play by…OUR rules.*** Not that there are any *rule books*. So it's just a matter of guessing is it? So he's wrong if he either doesn't know the rules, doesn't abide by them or care less what they are?

- ***…to have rules…why?*** So we're in command, in control, steering the ship….o….k….men should blindly follow…ah….ha….all tightly packaged. Oh yeah, I forgot we have superior knowledge and understanding about how love works.

- ***We are first priority to them and they shouldn't expect same from us?*** We're so used to looking out for ourselves and pushing for what we want in business that sometimes the same notion seems to slip in to our personal lives. If we're not careful, the potential love of our lives might get lost amongst all the other appointments and priorities.

- ***All ducks to be neatly in a row, ready for our arrival***…didn't know there was a pre-approved 'life situation' that a man needed to be in, to be a good prospect. I'd prefer to buy some new furniture!

It's certainly a little hard to see how love finds a spot in amongst all of these expectations. It's all somewhat unromantic isn't it?

I seem to have spent a lot of time over the past few years being privy to the group hyper-analysis of conversations, facial expressions, signals (imaginary or real), tones of voice and more, which more times than not leads my friends to the conclusion that this latest guy probably isn't right for them, so better off without.

Not bagging a bit of gossip here….we all love some of that.

But maybe if we spent less time pulling apart last night's activities and more time planning our next encounter with that special someone we'd worry less and enjoy more.

What do you think?

Does any of this ring true for you?

Isn't it about time we tried a little live and let live?

So what *does* your ultimate guy need to look like, to be like?

How perfect does he need to be to meet your criteria?

It's ok to have some standards, sure. You like a sense of humor…or…someone who enjoys water sports…..or someone who loves winter getaways.

Great! They're good things to spark a mutual interest.

But have we gone way beyond that?

Are we simply making it too hard for anyone to enter our lives, because it's just easier or *safer* that way?

The old saying 'paralysis by analysis' really shifts up a gear when you spend your time pulling apart every piece of a person, just to make conversation.

When does it come to the point where it's easier to reject than to expose ourselves to the rejection firing line?

When we're fresh and new on the dating scene, everything's exciting and fun. We start off a little shy and then as we get to know ourselves and become more confident in social settings, we savor a little risk.

Where down the line did we change from those bright sparks floating with the summer breeze, open to new experiences and excitement, to becoming jaded, closing down, shutting off.

It might be easier to protect ourselves, but it's a damn site lonelier.

LISTS…

...PLEASE NOT THE LISTS

Since when did we start making lists?

When you were eighteen did you have a list of every possible attribute or accessory a guy might need to have to be up to scratch?

Maybe you preferred blue eyes to brown or no chest hair.....but it was all a bit of fun wasn't it?

Have you noticed our lists usually now contain a host of material effects.....$$, house/s, car/s, you name it.

All too often they contain *preferred* occupations.....and worse....occupation types that are OUT....no matter what.

Run that by me again?

Is that a job description or a life partner we're talking about?

WE DON'T NEED MEN...............?

Sorry. Are we joking here?

This ridiculous, sad, backward notion, and the fact that anyone has intimated it let alone written books about it really gets my temperature rising.

Give me a break and get off the pogo stick before you damage something.

CAVEAT HERE…..I do understand that we as modern, sophisticated women are CAPABLE of running our lives by ourselves. That's fantastic. No complaints from me about earning a big pay packet and having my own stuff

…just…who'd want to do it alone?

If you're single and in your thirties or forties and you're reading this 'no men' stuff and it's making you feel better because you haven't found your guy yet, please, please get rid of it.

It's about the WORST thing you could be soaking up given you have now stated *for the record* that you want 'the life'.

I really understand that there are a lot of women who may not find the right man for them and need to look after their security, their future, their own lives.

Absolutely, 100%.

I just don't want to see their hope destroyed by people who have had a bad experience at some stage that has provoked them to put the man-free zone ideas together.

So I'll make my position clear.

I'm here to state FOR THE RECORD that not only
do I need men in my life, I want them and I love
'em.

And I don't mean I necessarily want to jump 'em.

I'm talking about real love.

For me, men are the most beautiful, funny,
thrilling, creative, loving, enjoyable people to have
in my life, and I wouldn't have it any other way.

I love the way they want to kid around, play
games, have fun, get together for a laugh, chill
out….they can find fun in anything, and to be
honest, I think we women sometimes lose a bit of
that kid humor and spontaneity to our detriment.

Instead of trying to *change* them, can't we just
enjoy them as we were created to?

Enjoy the differences…how boring would life be if
we were all the same?

Enough said.

I'll leave that one up to your own personal taste,
but hey lighten up and have a look at the plethora
of great things we can experience with and about
men.

And you know what?

If we're so into our standards, rules and lists let's
get it straight here. When all is said and done and

they've finished kidding around, men achieve great things anyway!

Look around at who the majority of really successful people are…in any fields from cooking to business to art….they just do it differently.

Often with a smile and a laugh.

We could now go in to a lengthy discussion on why there are more financially successful men than women. Equality, glass ceilings etc.

Let's not.

You and I both understand that.

I just think it's worth acknowledging the fact that men follow their own paths, in their own ways with or without us handing out our rulebooks.

So get with the program.

Start…celebrating our differences and finding fascination in the ways of men.

Start…treating men with the same respect and friendship you want to receive.

Stop…overanalyzing….
you're not their psychologist or mother.

Open the door.

Take some risk.

**AND
PLEASE
THROW AWAY
YOUR LIST!**

**AND START
MAKING
A NEW ONE!**

**ABOUT
YOU.**

CHAPTER 5 –

FOIBLES AND FAIRYTALES

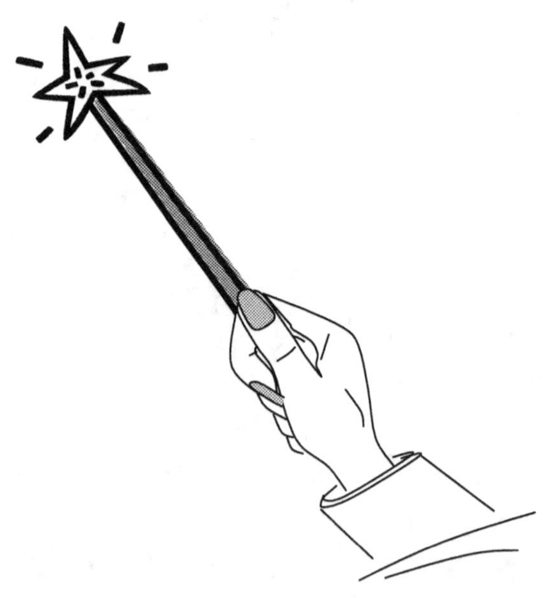

<u>**"WHO WOULD HAVE ME?"**</u>

When a successful thirty-something female fashion designer said this to me, you had to pick ME up off the floor. I was pretty stunned.

Attractive, funny, successful…..miserable, lost, scared.

She was having a hard time meeting available men, let alone getting relationships to last beyond the first couple of encounters.

And of course she was blaming herself for her low hit rate.

Do you think it was too much that I replied that given she works in Gaysville it might be a little difficult to meet Mr Straight?

Fashion parties are not exactly renown for a high percentage of hetero guys.

I just meant that she might want to mix it up a bit with different groups of friends, gay and straight, inside and outside her industry if she was keen to meet her mate.

Not very subtle sometimes am I?

So who would have you?

The guy you love spending time with.

The man you enjoy helping to fix the sink, just to be around him.

The lover you never want to let go of.

That's who'll have you.

Come on….pull out the pens and paper and write them down.

I want to see ALL the great things about you.

A warm-and-fuzzy request, maybe.

Essential, yes.

A nice long list covering all the different aspects and qualities of *you*.

(Fill out Checklist 1 to create your own personal list – see appendix!)

You're probably being a little tough on yourself right about now. We women seem to be harsh on ourselves on a regular basis!

So I want *YOU* to tell *YOU* how great *YOU* are.

Read it over a couple of times.

You **are** great!

Life's great!

If *YOU* don't believe in *YOU* it'll be that much harder for others to argue otherwise.

*****

<u>WHAT YOUR BEST FRIEND WON'T TELL YOU</u>

If you're reading this book and you're the married friend who just wants to help their pal find a mate but you can't quite say it all for fear of upsetting her, simply hand her this book and say "you're my friend and I love you, so GO GET A LIFE".

Hopefully she'll take it with your good intentions, and you'll be double dating in no time.

If on the other hand you have received this book from your married friend it means you need to

ACT NOW, WITHOUT HESITATION,

or you're gonna miss the boat.

Or if you've picked up this book yourself and have a best friend who's been single as long as you, there's something we need to discuss.

Your single friend probably won't tell you to 'get a life' because she likes you

'just the way you are'.

I've witnessed on a number of occasions the backlash from single best friends when their buddy tries to change.

You're their rock, their life line.

You see them most days.

They are heavily dependent on you for their social
life, their evening meal and their gossip.

Sometimes it's not in their best interests for you to
be happy with a husband and children because
where does it leave them?

They don't consciously *mean* it, but they
subconsciously *do* it.

Or, they might just not *get* him…..get what *you see*
in him.

I mean if we all liked the same person it'd be a bit
awkward!

I'm not saying they'll actively stop you from being
happy, but how often have they bagged the new
guy you're seeing because

     'he's not good enough for you'

or because *they* don't particularly like his
personality.

You're not twelve.

Work it out for yourself.

Is he a good guy or not?

She might be right, but she also might be wrong.

If I'd listened to one of my friends I might still be
desperate and dateless.

Yes I heard her message, but I made my own decision.

The best decision OF MY LIFE!

Sure, if your best friend is solidly behind your decision to 'get a life', fantastic….two heads are better than one.

But if not….get on with it anyway.

You don't have time to waste.

*****

PC, THE TRUTH BE TOLD

Ahhh political correctness.

The scourge of the 1990's.

Nothing hides the truth better than an excuse to talk around a subject.

An example :

One night I'm sitting in the back of a taxi with a woman. We'd just gone to see a mutual gal pal who looked fantastic after dropping some weight, getting some sleep and looking after herself.

I had known my friend since we were teenagers while this woman was a former work colleague.

The Career That Ate My Life

So being an old friend, I didn't hesitate to comment how great she'd looked. I had been worried about her because she had been overweight, dark around the eyes and looking pretty unhealthy.

In fact I was very excited that she had taken hold of her life with both hands and decided she wanted to change how she looked and how she felt.

Rather than joining me in rejoicing over our friend's transformation, my taxi companion set about telling me how mean I was to have mentioned our friend had been carrying too much weight.

I was pretty shocked.

And I was interested in the backlash.

Had I been too direct about my friend's past weight and health issue?

Or had I triggered an insecurity in my taxi companion?

I never did find out. But my friend continued on her 'look after self' campaign and looks great to this day.

So I'm not particularly worried about the backlash.

If you rely on your friends or family for advice and they're veering on PC, chances are they're not being *completely* honest with you.

What does that mean?

Are they lying to you?

Not really.

There's no malice intended.

They're just not being *straight* with you.

But that's life isn't it? Don't all of us skirt around issues at some time or another?

Sure.

Absolutely.

But there's polite and there's PC.

A big difference.

It comes down to thought process and intent.

If my old friend had asked me whether she was looking her best when she wasn't, I personally would have found a polite way of letting her know there was room for improvement, and then offered to help her come up with positive ways to change the areas of her life she was concerned about.

On the other hand, if she'd posed the same question to her former colleague, my guess is she would have received an answer something along the lines of …

"No, you're great. That's just you and if people don't like it that's their problem!"

…even though that may not have been what her friend was really thinking.

An intent to help versus an intent to smooth over a sticky subject and prop the person up.

That's how I read it anyway.

And where does that intent come from?

While there's no conscious malice, is there a subconscious reinforcement of her colleague's needs and padding down of insecurities?

If your inner circle of friends keep you as you are, does it make them feel more secure in some way?

So which friend would you prefer to have around?

Pick me! Pick me!

There are polite ways of helping your loved ones with their problems without making out that everything should stay just as it is.

Or if you're asking a question but really requesting the 'right' response then that's what you'll get nine times out of ten.

So have a think about who you're asking the questions to and why you're asking them.

And next time you talk with your friends about their jobs and their love lives I want you to take note of something.

The Career That Ate My Life

How often do you skim at the edges?

You don't lie to your friends. I mean you don't
make up stories and you're a dependable person.
But how often do you bend the truth so you don't
hurt their feelings?

We talked about your friends doing this to you, so
why wouldn't you unintentionally be doing it to
them?

Typical scenario :

Caroline's just been dumped by Markus after seven
weeks of patchy dating.

She's grown two dress sizes in six months because
she's been eating pizza every night at 9pm while
she's working long hours on a project when her
colleagues are all out the door by 6pm.

The conversation :

Markus dumped Caroline, so he's a creep.
Caroline's doing really well at work....she's such a
smart and successful person.
You love the new dress she's wearing – she looks
great in it.
And no her skin doesn't match the sickly grey
color of the office walls.

How much of that is true?

And how much have you said to support your
friend so as not to hurt her feelings?

Or are you a better friend if you gently tell her that she needs to cut back on the pizza, leave work at a reasonable hour and start jogging so she doesn't have a heart attack when she's forty-three?

It's ok to soften the edges when we're trying to help a friend.

But if Caroline really wants to get 'the life' we both know she needs to make some drastic changes or it just ain't gonna happen.

And if you're a really great friend and have the time, then pick her up a couple of mornings a week for a run that'll help you with your quest for 'the life' as well.

The moral of the story is don't be afraid to help your friends towards their goals and don't expect they're currently doing the same for you!

If we continue walking down this PC road we're going to have more and more people hiding behind excuses. Truth will become lost in falsehoods.

Or will it?

There's only so long you can hide from *inner* truth no matter how much you want to believe the bunkum other people fill you with.

SO TO HELL WITH POLITICAL CORRECTNESS!

One last word about emotional baggage.

The Career That Ate My Life

How many *ISSSSSSUES* can one have?

It's easy to weigh ourselves down with self-analysis and group discussions about everything that's wrong with us.

In reality, that type of conversation really leads nowhere unless we get something positive out of it.

A friend of mine was confiding her relationship woes in an acquaintance who responded that she regarded her as the 'complete package'.

And my pal was pretty happy about that. It made her feel reassured that her various attributes made her hot property in someone else's eyes.

My first reaction was 'huh?'

I just didn't get it.

Let me tell you that everyone's the complete package. There are just lots of different packages with lots of cool, unique, quirky idiosyncrasies.

We shouldn't need to be told.

We all have times when we feel less confident in ourselves and often when we see everyone else hooking up we can feel way out in left field.

But honey, you've got it all, like everyone else.

*****

WHERE 'BRIDGET JONES' WENT WRONG

We all love the Bridget Jones movies.

Every single girl's dream to have Hugh Grant and Colin Firth fighting over them and liking them 'just the way they are'.

Colin Firth can see right through our rough shod exterior to our scintillating personality in one fell swoop.

Minor point here.

IT'S A MOVIE….A FANTASY!

Yes it's true that when we get to know someone well we see beyond the aesthetic and understand the true and underlying beauty that makes that person extra special.

But if *we're* spending our time hyper-analyzing our prospective mate's big nose, ugly furniture or poor choice of trainers, can we honestly expect guys to instantly see beyond our facades if we're overtired, dressed like our nanna or have salt-and-pepper colored hair because we've been too busy to visit the hairdresser?

Ladies there is no denying we are up against it here if we don't take responsibility for our aesthetic.

That's not to say that everyone needs to look like Cindy Crawford.

But if we're not committed enough to our outward appearance, are we limiting our opportunities to move to that second stage with our new someone?

We are in our thirties or forties, blustering in late from a business meeting, dressed in our filing cabinet grey suits, and more concerned with what some work colleague said to upset us than how our man is.

And we're competing against that twenty-four year old chic at the other end of the bar with the spray-on tan, glistening teeth and carefree attitude who's been checking out our man for the last half hour while we've been putting the final touches on a briefing paper.

Hold on, hold on, let me add in that she also has a degree in fine art and speaks French fluently.

We arrive with our briefcase in hand while *she* has NO BAGGAGE to speak of because *she* just wants to have some fun.

Who would you choose to spend the evening with?

That's not fair is it?

Or is it?

You've *chosen* the path, your actions, your behavior.

And can I just ask at this point that we remove 'BAGGAGE' from our vocabulary unless we're going on a holiday?

Can we honestly say we have had that much pain that we can't dump it at the terminal and move on into the sunshine?

Everyone has disappointments at some time and for some people these can be particularly huge.

It takes time to deal with what can be very distressing relational issues.

It's just not a great idea to dump them on the dinner table next to the bread rolls.

We really have to think about how much we allow ourselves to tattoo past hurt on our foreheads for no other reason than allowing ourselves to be open to future experiences once we're over the initial deep upset.

So while I'm sure our men will like us 'just the way we are' when they get to know us, let's take out a bit of travel insurance in the meantime.

And once we get to stage two…..

Nahhh sorry.

You thought I was going to say we can go back to letting ourselves go….nope, sorry.

I need a lifetime change from you here.

Care about yourself, your aesthetic for the rest of your life. You'll just feel A LOT better for it.

The great part about stage two is we can open ourselves up for who we are.

Expose the true us!

"NO WAY!!!!"

YES WAY.

That's where all the great stuff happens and we learn how interesting, fun and loving we can be and have it returned back to us in spades!

Yummy!

I love stage two.

CHAPTER 6 –
FAGS AND HAGS

The Career That Ate My Life

S pending every Saturday night with your collection of gay friends or a band of single girlfriends sound familiar?

We love them, listen to them, look after them when they're blue, and they do the same for us….any time of day or night.

Sorry to say this…..we can't **MARRY** them!

Take a look around you at your group of pals.

You go out to a bar with the good intentions of meeting a new guy who might be 'the one'.

But most nights you end up back at your friend's house throwing up in the bathroom or watching GREASE for the eighty-fifth time.

Your gay friends……wonderfully fun and the type of friends you can share most anything with.

But you're never gonna meet your guy if you're lounging all over your gay male friends 24x7!

Prospects either think you're not available or don't want to invade what is obviously a fun night for you and your close confidantes.

And here's something I've only learned very recently through some idle chatter.

Straight guys DO NOT want to become close friends with gay men.

Yep, I did not know that!

Thinking this must be a gross over-generalization or misconception, I asked around and came back with the same answers over and over.

Gay and straight, straight and gay.

Men love each other's company no matter what walk of life they come from, as long as they have common interests.

But when it comes down to close, confidential, long-term friendships, I repeat, Straight guys DO NOT want to become close friends with gay men.

Why?

It doesn't really make sense to us women because we have such wonderful multi-faceted friendships with our boys.

I'll tell you why.

Because men, while we sometimes don't believe it, think on many different levels.

For straight men to become real friends, they scout prospects like they would a girlfriend. And when they want to talk about the usual topics – cars, women, relationships (yes, they do), life change, future – they want to talk with a man with those same interests and motivations.

They will be very happy to have lasting friendships with gay men. But if a true friend is someone who you discuss your innermost thoughts with, there are just some fundamental things that gay and straight men don't have in common.

Need I say more?

You don't have to choose between your gay friends and your straight partner.

You just might not want to assume anymore that your guy wants to be with your friends all the time like you do.

Your girlfriends…..if you and your gals have been single for quite a while then one or more of you may be going through a relationship down patch at any one time.

Not uncommon or unreasonable.

It comes back to what we talked about before – blaming ourselves for everything under the sun.

But if your girlfriends are mid-way through a downward spin and have stopped applying the mascara, are dressed in a paper bag or have storm clouds in their eyes when you go out, it's less than likely you're gonna get any interest shooting across the room at *you or your gang.*

Sure it might make you look better compared with the rest of your circle…meow! But that group of guys at the bar is looking at ALL of you.

Judgment by association.

So don't dump your play pals in the corner like old dolls you've grown out of, just mix it up a bit. Find a few extra people to hang out with.

Do something different. And really decide whether your friends are being the best 'wing men' they can be…..because this is YOUR time to find 'the life'.

Be kind. Be selfish.

Speaking of being selfish…vanishing acts.

Have you ever noticed that when one of your pals does land a new guy, they vanish in to thin air for a few months until it all starts to fall over?

Or when you do decide to change your life, your solid group of foot soldiers suddenly amscray?

An amazing thing happened to my friend when she announced she was moving overseas to shake it up a bit.

Her large, caring, co-dependent group of single friends all-but vanished within weeks, as they quickly set about shoring themselves up, making sure they were ok if they did lose her.

All that time spent with those people who were so flaky they didn't even wait for her to board the plane before they stamped her out of their lives.

So have a think about whether you're investing just a little too much time in some of your friendships if they're not as rock solid as you had hoped.

CHAPTER 7 –

PERCEPTION IS REALITY

If others perceive you as being happy with yourself they'll want to be part of your life.

Someone once said to me the times she was most popular with men were the times she had heaps of interesting stuff going on.

People want to be part of fun, not part of pain.

Your behaviors, tone and topics of conversation provide people with a snapshot of you.

A few examples :

Seriously Brainy…No *Seriously*

Every one of us is brainy, savvy, intelligent to some degree. If you've survived the rough and tumble of a career, that usually means you have a gift, an intellectual bent, a canny mind.

Do you know how interesting it is to talk with someone whose mind is sharp and colorful?

And do you know how dull it is to sit and listen to someone who waxes lyrical about how stupendously smart they are?

Drives to a level of self confidence.

*****

Is that a Lipstick in your Pocket or are you just Happy to See Me?

Since when did it become the norm for women to BE men?

Have you noticed how much bravado is creeping in to women's conversations about their personal lives?

A comment I've heard a bit too often of late is
        "she really likes him and says it's the best sex she's ever had."

What I find amazing about this comment is it's….so blokish!

Ok, ok…..I know it's ok to talk about sex with your friends….I'm the sort of person who likes to keep the detail to myself.

And when you think back to the guys who have always bragged about sex, isn't it often those who actually don't get much?

So it's up to you to say what you want, but my male friends tell me it's a real turn off when women stand around bragging about their one-nighters and eight hour sex sessions.

Good luck to the guy who has to compete with that!

And if the aim of the game here is to get 'the life'….then I hate to say it but the guys I know are inherently traditional, and are not really gonna be thinking of us as good prospects long term if they're viewed as just another notch on the bedpost.

By traditional I don't mean barefoot and pregnant…although most guys really ain't that far away from that.

What I mean is they want to know they're gonna be 'THE MAN' in some way shape or form, whether that means bread winner, car fixer or chief chef.

"Ugghhh", you say.

Don't blame the messenger here.

Men may be more sophisticated, metro-sexual blah, blah, blah….but it takes more than a few fashion trends to change thousands of years of physiology.

And would you really want to?

*****

Dress Like You Care

Recently I tried a little experiment at my office.

Historically I'd worn suits to work most days – mainly pantsuits – occasionally skirts.

Black, cream, navy, slate.

It hadn't worried me my whole career. I always looked good, and felt like the outfit suited my 'professionalism'.

Now in this new office I entered into, the traditional attire I'd worn like a badge of honor didn't seem to fit…..with men.

Women…no problem.

In some ways I felt like I wasn't being noticed enough for my contribution, and in others I learned that some colleagues found me to be too straight forward, too hard, abrupt.

So I listened…and changed.

I threw the suits in to the back of the cupboard and replaced them with feminine skirts, boots, and camisole sweaters in a variety of colors and fabrics.

Almost instantly I was NOTICED.

I was ASKED MY OPINION.

I was TREATED LIKE I MATTERED …by the men.

Not surprising. I looked prettier.

But my demeanor changed too. I worked on softening it to suit my work environment, sure.

But it was more than that.

The Career That Ate My Life

I was more relaxed, happier, and more creative in my work. My passion for subjects seemed to grow, because I was allowing myself to bring my 'home' personality to work.

I had always strictly split the two.

I felt better about myself because I was wearing clothes that I would usually have kept for special occasions.

So I felt special ALL the time.

I felt like I looked GREAT, ALL THE TIME.

And once I started, I wanted more.

I WANTED to put more time into my hair and makeup.

I WANTED to go shopping for the latest outfit.

Once you take a bite of the pie you want to keep eating.

Whether it was me changing the clothes or the clothes changing me, life at work became a lot more enjoyable.

I felt free because I was wearing clothes that WERE ME, not suits that HID ME.

So everything was great, except for some of…The WOMEN.

Two things happened.

One positive, one negative.

The more junior female staff REALLY started to look up to me, asking me to mentor them, seeking my guidance.

The senior women, some of whom are unfortunately the primary ones who need to read this book, were NOT happy.

When it came time for peer review, those senior women set about attempting to undermine my credibility.

Lucky for me the MEN were in charge!

So what did I do?

I INCLUDED those negative women in my club.

I invited them in by talking about fashion with them, their shoes, their makeup, my hair, my skirts.

Because ALL WOMEN want to feel part of the beauty club. A lot just don't feel they'll be let in the front door.

So what's my point?

If you're wearing a business suit, work shoes, accessories, make sure they're fashionable.

Ill-fitted jackets and shoe styles that went out five years ago just don't cut it. In fact I think they do the opposite for us.

The Career That Ate My Life

When we wear suits like straight jackets we *can* come across almost ANDROGONOUS.

That's right. Our work clothes can knock out any sex appeal we have.

Sure you don't want to go to the other extreme of micro minis and low cuts to your navel.

But we ARE women.

We just happen to be BUSINESS WOMEN.

Why should we lose who we are because of our office dress code?

My point is, if your business wardrobe doesn't match your personality, or hides and hinders it in some way, now's a good time to spring clean.

Bring your LIFE into your WORK.

Even in the most traditional firms where suits and stockings are the requirement, a bright shirt, sexy shoes or a great hair style can really reflect your personality and add to your dimensions without you needing to open your mouth.

Every time you get dressed and do your hair and makeup, picture walking past your future boyfriend as the litmus test.

Would he find you attractive, sexy?

Would he notice you…at all?

CHAPTER 8 –

POWER, EQUALITY, SANTA CLAUSE

The Career That Ate My Life

The more we climb the mystical corporate ladder, the more we learn about true power in an organization and what to do to get it.

What a maze!

Our ambition continues to drive us on a campaign to achieve, and achieve and achieve.

And the lopsided male/female dominance in many organizations forces us to over-achieve, continuously, to get anywhere close to the salaries, perks and positions of our male counterparts.

Being the business success that you are, you've learned about, and are probably still baring the scars from, many situations you'd rather not have experienced.

The higher you go, the rougher it gets.

We're not talking about piddly little wages or small fry competition here. We're talking about you outshining and outmaneuvering people with high profiles, huge dollars at stake, large mortgages and massive egos.

So you come home, day in day out, having just sat through this scary stuff, and if you're not careful, that hunger, that push, that power charge starts to seep into your home life, to an unwilling recipient.

Here lies the deep contrast.

The conflicting co-existence of your two lives.

The Career That Ate My Life

You now slip in to your frock to relax with your
man, and you have to put all of this melee aside
and become the little woman.

Because your man has no idea that you go through
this kinda stuff.

No matter how many times or different ways you
express it, he has no real concept that that's what
you do….that you're a big wig.

No concept.

He just sees you looking cute in your frock.

He understands you have a good job and he's
proud of you….yep….and that's about it.

And while I still to this day *wish* that Santa Clause
existed, I know he lives in my 'little girl' thoughts.

So as much as I'd like to say that equality in
relationships exists, it really doesn't in *every*
aspect, only some, and probably never will.

Why?

Because we're built differently.

No matter how much perceived power you have in
your job, the fact is you're smaller, weaker and
have different attributes to your other half.

Men will always be bigger, stronger, tougher.

The Career That Ate My Life

For women, being tough in business should mean
you can take the hits when they happen.

It shouldn't mean you have to become man-like.

That only serves to us being called awful names by
our bullying colleagues.

Being tough in your personal life only brings
conflict and tears. Usually yours.

Whatever it is, men have to have a 'job' in the
relationship. It doesn't do much for the ego when
men constantly hear what they're doing wrong
from their woman.

Is it gonna kill you to let him open the door or walk
on the outside near the curb? I find it pretty cute
myself.

And he'll be more than happy if you're bringing in
a truck load of cash yourself, so don't worry about
having to give up everything to keep the right guy.

Nothing will make a man's heart sing more than
being your focal point, being cared for….even just
a little.

There's always a little bit of mother or carer
evident in any long lasting relationship I've ever
witnessed, like it or lump it.

So are you willing to leave your business life at the
door and somehow find the balance between home
and work?

FAIR? No Way

REALITY? Absolutely.

Want to change it? Always.

Able to change it? No chance in hell.

Roll with it or roll against it.

Just know it exists.

Whether it's in your words, actions or body
language, perception is reality.

It's up to you to create the world you want to live
in and that someone else wants to share with you.

Again let me stress you don't need to sacrifice all
you've achieved to get 'the life'.

But you do need to bring some of that beautiful
person out that's been pushed in under the power
suit for too long for people to see who you are
beyond your job title.

CHAPTER 9 – THE GAME

WORK IS A GAME.

RELATIONSHIPS ARE REAL.

NOT THE OTHER WAY ROUND.

L et me paint a picture for you.

You've built your solid career from the ground up.

You're professional, always doing excellent work and people know they can depend on you.

Meanwhile your male colleague is out having drinks and runs into a couple of the company directors who shout a few rounds.

He's a good enough type of guy…comes in late sometimes after a big night, makes the odd screw up, but generally does a good job.

It's promotion time….who gets the job? If you're really lucky, you do. If you work in many corporations….he does.

Why?

The reasons are obvious.

(1) he's a guy….like we've said, life and business isn't fair

(2) he's developed a solid network of relationships....it doesn't have to be about drinks with the boys either

(3) you've been focusing on looking 'professional', but how much do people know about your real personality?

Yep....a big generalization....and not something we need to dwell on except to say work, the office, is a game....and when you start treating it like a game it becomes much more fun, you don't get quite as heartbroken when things don't go your way, and you draw a line in the sand that allows you to focus on other things outside work, which in turn make you a more interesting and colorful person.

When you become more interesting and interested, you're easier to talk to and much more fun to be around.

Suddenly you're making those other girls look pretty one-dimensional, without having to show off how brainy you are.

How many times have we made the mistake of talking about work with a guy we're interested in?

I'm not talking about some chit chat. I mean a half hour one-sided talk fest about every explicit detail of your fantabulous career.

What's he reading in to this?
- She's boring
- She doesn't have time for me

- She freaks me out….how can I compete with that?

If you compete too heavily within your relationship, expect to be beaten and to potentially lose the whole race.

I myself have a non-compete policy with pretty-much everyone. I try to anyway. I prefer to compete against myself and achieve what's important to me.

Let me say it again….you don't have to give up the career….you just need to de-focus on it for five minutes while you're getting to know your soul mate ok?

But hey, let's just think about this for a moment.

Will I?

Ok. I'm just gonna say it.

SCREW THE CAREER

I've gone too far.

I can hear you say it….

"you mean to tell me you want to ditch everything I've worked on for the past ten-plus years??????"

If you want to get 'the life' you need to make a decision,

RIGHT HERE,

RIGHT NOW.

You have the cash in the bank, maybe the dream chattels already….but we've already established there ain't no bounty of men lining up to come inside.

It's you and the cat.

If you don't take a stand TODAY where do you think you're gonna end up?

My friend said to me :

	"I feel like I'm sitting at the bus stop and assuming the bus will turn up sooner or later….but I'm thirty-seven and thinking should I get a taxi?"

My response?

Forget the taxi, go catch the jet.

It's beyond time.

You have to grab this adventure with both hands and GO NOW.

Go where?

Go **somewhere** different.

Do **something** different.

Your routine is NOT working.

You need to change it in a big way now or face the likelihood that you and the cat will still be sitting in your apartment in five years, ten years time.

What are we talking about here?

That comes down to you and your journey.

The path you've taken to now is your own and you need to map out the next stage…now.

When I say 'screw the career' I don't mean you need to quit your job today.

I mean you need to break focus…take your foot off that work pedal and apply the fuel to your personal life.

You can still do your job….your professionalism is a *given*.

But you need to wrench back some of your time and energy out of the clutches of the almighty dollar or power ego….or both if you have two strikes against you.

Think about how much physical and mental energy you put in to your job every day and how little you have left by the time you get home.

You can barely open the mail that's piling up in the corner because your head's so chock full of information, emails, hallway gossip and data that you can't take on one more thing.

Just think how much your personal life could benefit if you transfer even 10% of that focus away from your job.

If you were twenty-five, 10% might be enough.

So compound that to your current age and you're talking about a SUBSTANTIAL ADJUSTMENT.

It may be for six months or it may be forever.

But ONLY YOU can determine how much you're willing to risk NOT getting 'the life'.

There is no silver bullet or fix-all remedy here.

You can't just push your life to the background and hope it will all sort itself out.

"Wake me when it's over" is not an option.

So whether you box your stuff in storage for six months and go work at a bar in Ibiza, move suburbs to a more family-friendly environment, take a job where you know there will be plenty of single guys or simply change pub haunts, your life is your own.

Get to it….go catch the jet.

CHAPTER 10 –

FEMINISM, FOR WHOM THE BELLE TOLLS

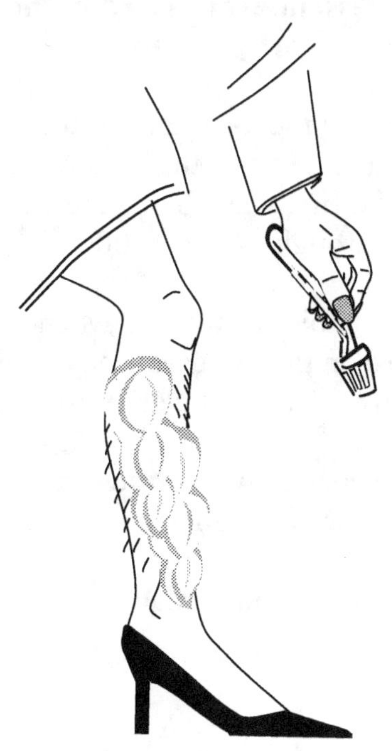

The Career That Ate My Life

Sista, sista. Did you ever think we'd be here?
Sista, sista. Could you ever see the lives you'd help
create? Could you ever see the difference you
would make?....

What a topic.

Where to start?

....the greatest revolution of women in
history....

....hairy legs and mono-brows.....

..screwed up and spat out....

....the quintessential 'F' word in the commercial
workplace today...

Let's go back to the dark ages of the 1960's &
1970's, and the dawn of the 'second wave' of
feminism (the first wave being the early progress in
late 1800's through to mid 1900's).

We were the babies of this era when options for
women were on the increase – easier divorces,
ability to earn a living, the drive for equality.

People were changing. Families were changing,
splitting, prospering, collapsing, evolving.

A profound and monumental era of liberation for
many.

The Career That Ate My Life

As this era developed into the 1980's and early 1990's, the vision, the agenda, the motivation sprawled across every topic imaginable.

The hunt for equality morphed into power suits, the take-no-prisoners attitude, the magazines that bleated career women 'had it all', the gender-less jobs…air hostesses became flight attendants, the postman became the post office worker.

"Nine to Five" and "Working Girl" were smash hit movies of the era, breaking new ground for the working woman. I still watch the re-runs for the zany hair and clothes. They're so much fun!

Over time, a menagerie of platforms began to emerge for anyone with an argument or agenda to take a stand, and DEMAND change.

So we, western society, changed…and changed.

Before long, equal naming conventions wasn't enough.

Let's go full throttle and just *blank out* every term that can mean anything so we have a purely gender-free, race-free, socioeconomic-free language.

The birth of political correctness.

As the soapbox revolution continued and hairy legs grew thicker, it was hard to see the forest for the trees and the corporate head honcho's became nervous.

The Career That Ate My Life

"We don't want disruptive, demanding staff. We want amiable, hard working people who'll earn what we want to pay them", they'd shout in the boardrooms.

So you and I, rising through the ranks in this era, had to decide which way to go.

I don't know about you, but somewhere down the line, *feminism* became a definite no-no topic for me and my female friends in the commercial workplace. You didn't champion the cause at work if you wanted to stay around let alone get promoted.

Not only that, because we had basically benefited from the blood, sweat and tears of our forebears, we actually didn't feel the need to bang the drum.

It was all there…readily available to us.

And the combination of all these changes and articles and guidance and wide scale misdirection lead us to the 'power woman' ideals, the career as everything.

I doubt our early feminist sisters would have ever thought we would end up painting ourselves into yet another corner where we have less *life* options in our sights just to gain more *career* options.

They would never have wanted a life for us that in some ways was *worse off* than when they started.

The scales have definitely dropped to the other extreme, and we're the ones weighing them down.

We need to rebalance the scales.

WOMEN NEED TO FIND THE BALANCE.

The stakes are HUGE.

We've bet the farm….and the farmer, and the kids that go along with it. If we don't change course NOW where might we end up?

Less smart women having kids means less smart kids and less kids in general, which skews the earning capability of the economy, meaning we're going to be working and paying dues well into our later years.

YUCK!

What happened to living out our years going for long beach walks, baking cakes for the local school fair and putting our feet up?

So let's define WHO WE WANT to BE.

We're not Feminists, but are we

Commercialists

– the new era of modern commercial womanhood that says…

> "I AM going to take back my *life*, my *priorities*, my *options*, and…

I AM gonna GET THE LIFE I WANT without having to throw away all I've worked for."

Where we define what we want….for ourselves.

The Commercialist

- New Feminism -

The 21st Century Business Woman.

CHAPTER 11 –

WOMEN – THE GREAT DIVIDE

The Career That Ate My Life

Have you ever noticed when you're at a party, say
a family and friends gathering like Christmas or an
engagement, that you have a slight query in your
head about where you fit in this picture?

There's cousin Rita in the corner, a homemaker
who you haven't seen since she's had the twins, so
you wander over for a chat.

Beyond a few minutes catch up and reminiscing,
there's silence. You draw on all your resources to
pull out a conversation from nowhere, just to keep
mouths moving and histories bonding.

What you're encountering is the unspoken divide
between women.

The homemaker, the career woman, the super
woman all move in silos of activity…circles that
barely brush the sides of each others' parallel
worlds.

Maybe you don't feel comfortable talking about the
whole family thing because you're not there yet
and you can't stand to be asked AGAIN when it's
all gonna happen for you.

Maybe your cousin feels uncomfortable because
she doesn't think there's really ANYTHING
eventful or worthwhile in her life that you would
understand or be interested in.

So she says nothing.

The Career That Ate My Life

And the superwoman buzzing around the room has
no time to talk with anyone unless she's followed
by a band of nannies….she's just way too busy.

We women are at times our own worst enemies.

We compartmentalize ourselves and think we can't
contribute to each others' quality of life.

You're the best person cousin Rita could talk to
about things outside her normal routine to get an
idea of what else is happening 'out there'.

Cousin Rita's the best person you could talk to
about real life. The stuff you just don't get enough
of when walking from the car park to the office.

And the superwoman is the best person both of you
can laugh with about the ludicrous amount of *stuff*
she has going on in her life.

She's either superhuman or super-tired, and
probably needs a battery recharge with some fun
company.

Our support for each other, our openness to learn
about each other and acceptance of each
other….without stigma and without labels….is our
greatest gift to each other.

It's easy to forget about cousin Rita until next
Christmas, but you can both gain so much if you
make the odd phone call or visit in between.

CHAPTER 12 – TIDAL WAVE

By now you're probably sitting there thinking a mixture of :

"I've made a huge mistake with my life!"

**"My friends are lying to me to
make me feel good!"**

**"I'm part of the biggest love drought
in living history!"**

...and...

"I'm the twenty-first century equivalent of..."

A SPINSTER!!!

There, we've said it. The last taboo has now been broken.

Stop right there.

Technically, you're correct.

You're on your own, and not by conscious choice.

BUT

That doesn't mean your fate has to be that of two skeletons found in an apartment....one human, one feline.

Put a smile on your face....I want to see a really big grin.

Because guess what…you're now *committed* to sorting this out *once and for all.*

Forget about tagging yourself with the 'S' word. That's just too harsh and too last-century.

Push that stigma behind you and move on.

Forget who you are right now, just for a moment.

Have a think back to when you were a kid and life was pretty hassle-free. No responsibilities besides making your bed or taking out the garbage.

Then think about what you were like when you were at your twenty-first birthday.

You were probably working or finishing off study…plenty of friends around….lots of cute guys who thought you were even cuter….and life was pretty much a fun park.

Those sentimental memories are great, but you need to decide that it's not time to become twelve or twenty-one again.

Don't use your past to show you what you lack in the present. Use it to your advantage to help you remember your true self and what really makes you happy.

By reflecting back on the best aspects of your life *then* and who you were *then,* let it help you reassess who you are *now* and what you want *now.*

How did you get so caught up in all the 'wrong' things?

Guess what. It doesn't matter. It's your past, not your present.

It happens in what seems like an instant, but it's taken you *years and years* to get to where you are from where you were then.

You're not the girl expectantly waiting to be asked to dance at the prom or giddy after another night of outrageous partying.

And you don't need to be.

You can't *change* the past or *live* in the past. But you can *understand* and *accept* the past for all that it's given you.

If you want to know what a big mistake is, it's sitting around pondering 'if only'.

Don't make that mistake.

So who are you?

You are history in the making.

Pretty cool when you think about it isn't it?

You are a living, breathing history of your experiences to date, and the course you set from now will guide the rest of your journey.

Your portrait is not yet finished.

Your book is only half read.

It's not too late.

It's time to be thirty-four, thirty-nine, forty-two.

And let's do it with style.

It's your time.

It's your right to decide your destiny.

CHANGE COURSE NOW.

This is not a time to be scared….to stand frozen while the tidal wave looms above your head.

This is the time to dive straight through that wave and come up to the surface into the sun.

*****

__ENERGY__

Energy is the buzz word of the new millennium.

Whether you're religious, spiritual or scientific, the common thread for us all is that what you put in you get back in spades.

What does that mean?

The Career That Ate My Life

It means that if you concentrate your energy, your focus, your mind on what's *wrong* with your life, what you *don't* have and how *bad* things are, you'll continue to attract what you focus on.

So the more we criticize ourselves, our surroundings or worry ourselves about the future, the more we reinforce that position.

Way back at the start of this book we allowed ourselves a little room to worry in order to focus some attention and urgency on the situation at hand.

But it's graduation day. You're now way past that point and are ready to face this situation head on.

The big difference between who you were when we started our journey and now is that you're breaking through your own personal tidal wave and are ready to paddle out into the deep blue.

So how do we break free from negativity once and for all?

It may seem trite, but we need to focus on what's great about our lives, and lift ourselves up out of the hole we've worked so hard to dig.

By harnessing energy and directing it to what you want and where you want to be, you replace that closet full of straight jackets – fear, anger, ego, sorrow – with plenty of space for love, joy and happiness.

*****

<u>UNLOCK YOUR FUTURE</u>

What time is it you may ask?

Whether it's past time or in good time, it's now the right time for you to stage an INTERVENTION …. ON YOU.

Ah ha….an intervention like the ones you do for a drug addict, alcoholic….except this time *you're* deciding that *your* career obsession has to change.

Sit down and assess your life….I'm talking all aspects.

(Refer List 1 to help you complete your assessment – see appendix!)

Work, friends, family, experiences, fitness, outer beauty, inner beauty, goals, likes, dislikes, men you go for…or don't….

And GET REAL.

If you expect to marry a male supermodel or an Einstein with a seven figure bank balance you'd better expect to put up your end of the bargain!

Now what we could dive into here is hyper-analysis and a date with the bottle if we take this the wrong way.

If this isn't a positive and enlightening experience for you then throw your initial self-assessment away and start again.

And GET HUMAN.

"What the hell is she talking about?"

I'm talking about finding ways to really touch and connect with other people.

The cousin Rita's.

How long is it since you spent a good length of time with your parents, brother or old friend from school who really know you and really love you?

How long is it since you were actually around kids or could remember feeling comfortable around babies?

It took me FOREVER to feel like babies were truly…*people*, and then this wonderful thing happened where I started to really love them…

Don't know why it happened but I really started to notice all their little nuances and see that they're really fun and interesting to be around. I suppose it's good old cluckiness!

If you want 'the life' you gotta be around people who are LIVING IT, not people who are LOOKING FOR IT.

Why is this all so hard?

We're used to winning in business, so why aren't we winning *the way we want to* in life?

Put it this way…if you're working on a key campaign and somewhere during the project you find a major flaw in the customer data, you have three options.

Stop the campaign…kill it.

Go ahead with what you have….risk it.

Fix the data, adjust the campaign and possibly delay launch a few weeks….and win.

So use everything you have to WIN.

The changes you make today will provide a great boost to your life, no matter what the outcome.

YOU HAVE NOTHING TO LOSE.

"But I have everything to lose".

YOU HAVE *ABSOLUTELY* NOTHING TO LOSE.

Look at the next six months of your life and what's planned.

Talk with your family about giving you some guidance and support.

And let them know it's your NUMBER ONE PRIORITY to 'get a life'.

That's right NUMBER ONE.

Anything less and you are far less likely to make any really meaningful change.

BUILD YOUR TEAM.

I know it's tough enough to confront yourself with the facts, so speaking with your family or friends about such a sensitive topic ain't easy either.

It's like you're admitting 'failure' in your life when you're used to being the perfect shining star who everyone admires for 'having it all'.

It really depends on how you decide to view and communicate your situation. A problem or an opportunity?

Think about what works for you. You've pushed along this far by yourself and how has that worked out?

You may really need or want a team to help you deliver your own personal campaign.

Just make sure you pick the 'right' team that wants to help you as much as you want to be supported. Why do it alone?

*****

<u>LET'S GET IT STRAIGHT</u>

If I haven't made it quite clear enough until now, let me be straight forward here.

BELIEVE IN YOURSELF

BE KIND TO YOURSELF

HARNESS YOUR ENERGY AND MAKE IT WORK *FOR* YOU, NOT *AGAINST* YOU

BE HAPPY AND THANKFUL FOR WHO YOU ARE AND WHAT YOU HAVE RIGHT NOW

DECIDE TODAY TO TURN NEGATIVE THOUGHTS INTO DELICIOUSLY HAPPY THOUGHTS

FOCUS ON YOUR GREAT ATTRIBUTES

STOP PULLING MEN APART WITH ANALYSIS AND CRITICISM, JUST TO MAKE CONVERSATION

LOVE OTHER PEOPLE FOR WHO THEY ARE, NOT WHAT BOXES THEY TICK IN YOUR CHECKLIST

CLEAR OUT THE CLOSET OF YOUR
MIND, READY TO FILL IT WITH
NEW AND EXCITING ADVENTURES

TAKE ACTION NOW FOR POSITIVE CHANGE.

*****

THE GREAT TRANSFORMATION

A final activity.

Tell me this.

Where is your mind focused?

Where is your heart focused?

Now with all you've learned, align mind to heart.

Easy isn't it?

Now just do that for a lifetime.

It's that easy and it's that difficult.

The great transformation of your life has begun.

*****

<u>ONE FOR THE ROAD</u>

As we sip our cocktails this fine evening before you depart on your great adventure, I just want to say *thank you*.

Thank you…for coming on this journey with me.

For allowing me to share my thoughts with you.

And if you're saying thanks back to me…no sweat.

What are friends for?

Go catch the jet…

…and send me a postcard.

*****

THE END

*****

APPENDIX

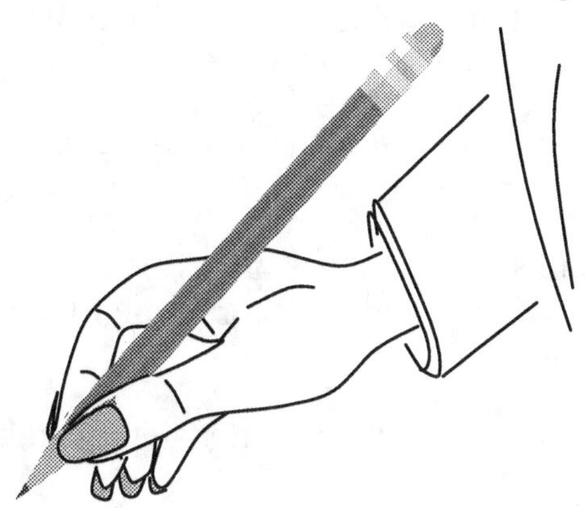

<u>Quiz 1 – How deep in the career hole are you?</u>

Rate the following statements, giving yourself a score of 1-5, 5 being the highest :

1. I frequently work back at the office. I have a picture of the sun at my desk to remind me of what it looks like.

2. My last significant boyfriend was in the twentieth century.

3. I exercise every leap year.

4. I spend an inordinate amount of time with people I can't marry due to their gender or gender-bender status.

5. There are so many notches on my bedpost that it looks like someone attacked it with a hack saw.

6. There are so few notches on my bedpost that my parents bought me a male escort as a gift for my last birthday.

7. People say I have balls. I often get asked how they're hanging.

8. My favorite topics of conversation are (a) my day; (b) my latest promotion and (c) my new Prada briefcase.

9. My wine bill is as big as my tax bill.

10. I met my kitchen for the first time the other day.

Now add your scores.

How did you rate?

0-10	Girl, what are you reading this book for?
10-20	You're doing ok NOW, but are you sure you want to board that runaway train?
20-35	Wrong way, go back! You're speeding head first towards the edge!
35-50	Mayday! Mayday! Train wreck! Call in the rescue helicopter with an extra-long ladder and flashlight. We're going deep underground

<u>Checklist 1– What's great about me?</u>

Here's a list to point you in the right direction and remind *you* what's great about *you*!

Tick the boxes that are appropriate to you and add more attributes in the blank spaces below.

Feel great about yourself!

Attribute	✓	Attribute	✓	Attribute	✓
Hair		Funny		Giving	
Face		Quirky		Honest	
Eyes		Serious		Cute	
Lips		Humorous		Fit, healthy	
Nose		Colorful		Sweet	
Breasts		Sophisticated		Simply nice	
Navel		Approachable		Opinionated	
Torso		Happy		Clever	
Buttocks		Generous		Great friend	
Hands		Sassy		Curious	
Feet		Intelligent		Holistic	
Legs		Kind		Nurturing	
Skin		Loving		Balanced	
Petite		Adventurous		Crazy	
Tall		Modern		Cool	
Cuddly		Sporty		Great fun	
Voluptuous		Great talker		Fair	
Slim		Great listener		Charming	
Cheeky		Naughty		Vivacious	
Shy		Class act		Intelligent	
Spiritual		Calm		Wildfire	

Now write yourself a love letter!

____

____

____

____

<u>List 1– My life assessment.</u>

Here's a table of life subjects to point you in the
right direction and help you assess where you're at
and what you want from life.

Fill in the table below. Score yourself from 1-10,
10 being the highest, on how close you are to
where you want to be.

Subject	Where I am now	Where I want to be	Score 1-10
Health & fitness			
Personal Appearance			
Personal Demeanor			
Family Relationships			
Relationships with Friends			

Social Life & Activities			
Love Life & Marriage			
Inner Beauty & Strengths			
Outer Beauty & Strengths			
Personal Goals			
Work & Career			
Life Experiences			
Other Key Areas			

Now choose three priority areas from your list that you want to start work on straight away :

1. ______________________________
2. ______________________________
3. ______________________________

For each of the three priority areas chosen, write down the next step you'll take towards your goal.

1. ______________________________
   ____
2. ______________________________
   ____
3. ______________________________
   ____

Set yourself a target completion date for each of the next steps and mark those dates on your calendar.

Now go to it!

If you do build your own personal team to help you on your journey, make sure you let them know what your goals and priorities are and how they can support you to achieve them.

If you want to be totally out there, stage your own intervention and invite your team to participate!

Good luck!

Journal

Keep a journal of your journey to remind you where you started and how far you've come!

Date	Notes

<u>Notes</u>

<u>Notes</u>

<u>About the Author</u>

Patricia McGovern is a business executive with twenty years of wide ranging commercial experience.

Patricia's vast personal insights into the workings of the corporate ladder have been developed throughout her career across media, telecommunications and financial services.

Holding commerce and journalism degrees along with a number of professional affiliations, Patricia enjoys balancing her business life with her creative interests.

If you would like to send Patricia a postcard of your own journey, you can contact her at pmcgovern01@gmail.com.

*****

The Career That Ate My Life

9 781847 535344